# Diamonds For Daily Living

## Words For Winning At Life

## J. KONRAD HÖLÈ

Proverbs 4:7 says, "Wisdom is the Principle thing." Wisdom is the only proof that you are being **"Mentored"** by the **"Most Intelligent Person In The Universe,"** the **"Holy Spirit."**

Unless otherwise indicated, all Scripture quotations are taken from the King James Version of the Bible.

*Diamonds for Daily Living*

Copyright © 1996 by J. Konrad Hölè
ISBN 1-888696-00-1
World Centre Ministries
P.O. Box 41010
Minneapolis, MN 55441

Published by
The World Press
P.O. Box 41010
Minneapolis, MN 55441

# Foreword

I realized that the closer I became to the **"Holy Spirit,"** who is the **"Spirit of Wisdom,"** not only would He teach me everything He knows, but He would ignite a craving within me to know more. You will never remember someone's **"Words,"** as much as you will remember someone's **"Point."** That is why I wrote this book. It is simply because I believe that one **"Diamond Key"** of wisdom can unlock a **"Vaulted Treasure"** of information.

You and I are only ever **"One Truth"** away from what we do not understand, and what we need to know. These are not copies of someone else's quotes, or revelation. These are **"Diamonds of Revelation"** that the "Holy Spirit" has unlocked to me in Crusades, Seminars, and Teachings around the world. Feel free to share these with someone that needs to know what you know.

**Diamonds** are not just a **"Girl's Bestfriend,"** they're everybody's **"BESTFRIEND."**

Enjoy.

J. Konrad

# Dedication

This collection of **"Diamonds"** is dedicated first and foremost to: My **"Incredible Wife"** Kristina, whose merciful, graceful, and peace-making nature graciously balances out the perfectionist driven, absolutely decisive, and always opinionated volcano that she married! If I had it to do over again, I'd still pick you. You're wonderful.

My **"Dearest Friend and Mentor,"** Dr. Mike Murdock who would always tell me, "If you can't get to the point, don't go on the journey." Thank you, MM, for teaching me how to get to the **"Point"** so quickly.

And most of all, my most **"Precious Companion,"** the **"Holy Spirit,"** who patiently and gently does not stop polishing **"My Coals,"** until they become **"His Diamonds."** You're the Greatest!

# Table of Contents

# Table of Contents (cont.)

# Table of Contents (cont.)

# Accusation

**1** **Accusation** is your enemy's way of influencing your future, by intimidating your present.

**2** The moment you expose an **Accusation**, you disarm the source.

**3** Your response to **Accusation,** determines how far off course your enemy can detour you.

**4** Those on their way to the fight, talk different than those already in the ring.

**5** **Accusation** can only go as far as fact.

**6** False **Accusation** will only be as successful as other peoples ability to interrogate truth.

**7** Those who do not embrace truth, entertain a lie.

---

D i a m o n d    W o r d s

*Who, when he was reviled, reviled not again; when he suffered, he threatened not; but committed himself to him that judgeth righteously: I Peter 2:23*

# Achieving

**Achievers** think silently, before they speak loudly.

**Achievers** plan carefully, before they build largely.

**Achievers** examine practically, before they react wisely.

**Achievers** pursue intently, before they decide directionally.

**Achievers** interrogate deeply, before they commit relationally.

**Achievers** observe privately, before they react publicly.

**Achievers** test indefinitely, before they trust loyally.

---
## Diamond Words

*The soul of the sluggard desireth, and hath nothing: but the soul of the diligent shall be made fat. Proverbs 13:4*

---

# Adversity

**1** **Adversity** expands your threshold of endurance.

**2** **Adversity** magnifies your position for promotion.

**3** **Adversity** increases your borders of potential.

**4** **Adversity** is used by your enemy as a "Crisis" and by *God* as a "Classroom."

**5** Your reaction to someone in **Adversity**, determines *God's* reaction to yours.

**6** **Adversity** begins the ride on the "Curve of Change."

**7** **Adversity** is not an enemy, it's just proof you have one.

---

**————— D i a m o n d    W o r d s —————**

*When thou passest through the waters, I will be with thee; and through the rivers, they shall not overflow thee: when thou walkest through the fire, thou shalt not be burned; neither shall the flame kindle upon thee. Isaiah 43:2*

# Anger

1. You will never change anything you don't hate.

2. Your **Anger** is a link to the problems, *God* has called you to solve.

3. Release your **Anger** when it's a "Puff," not an "Explosion."

4. Be a "Victor," not a "Victim."

5. **Anger** is the revealer of fear.

6. Uncontrolled **Anger**, is the proof of unresolved hurt.

7. Have enough fortitude to pick a side, and enough conviction to walk on it.

---
D i a m o n d     W o r d s

*Be not hasty in thy spirit to be angry: for **Anger** resteth in the bosom of fools. Ecclesiastes 7:9*

---

# Anointing

**1** The **Anointing** is the bridge between the impossible and the possible.

**2** The more of *His* presence you allow around you, the more of *His* **Anointing** will flow through you.

**3** The **Anointing** makes you a carrier of someone else's Miracle!

**4** If you never know the *Holy Spirit*, you will never know how much of *His* power you contain.

**5** Anything that offends the *Holy Spirit*, will offend *His* **Anointing**.

**6** The **Anointing** will defend any covenant promise *God* said you had a right to.

**7** Reverence the **Anointing**. When something is a treasure, it will be a pleasure.

---

D i a m o n d      W o r d s

*The Spirit of the Sovereign Lord is on me, because the Lord has **Anointed** me... Isaiah 61:1*

# Appearance

1. People will see you, before they hear you.

2. Look good to yourself. You can't win if you feel like a loser.

3. Get a photograph of where you want to be physically, financially, fashionably, and intellectually, and build every day around it.

4. Your **Appearance** is the platform for your presentation.

5. Study "Class." Sloppiness is not an excuse for individuality.

6. Never give others the "true **Appearance**" of "false information."

7. **Appear** reachable. No one will reach for you, if they don't believe they can touch you.

---
**— D i a m o n d    W o r d s —**

*A merry heart maketh a cheerful countenance: but by sorrow of the heart the spirit is broken*
*Proverbs 15:13*

---

# Assignment

**1** Your **Assignment** is proof *God* planned for you to succeed in something.

**2** When you're out of your **Assignment**, deception becomes rational, and error becomes probable.

**3** If *God* could have found a replacement for your **Assignment**, *He* would have never given it to you.

**4** Your **Assignment** is proof *God* preserved you, in order to preserve *His* purpose in you.

**5** Your **Assignment** will either be promoted, or distracted by a person.

**6** Never defend your **Assignment** to someone with a different one.

**7** If your life is not over, then neither is your **Assignment.**

---

D i a m o n d    W o r d s

*...the law is not made for a righteous man, but for the lawless and disobedient, for the ungodly and for sinners...   I Timothy 1:9*

---

# Associations

**1** The seed you sow in others will determine the harvest you reap from them.

**2** Never link yourself to those walking outside their assignment.

**3** Those walking in disobedience, attract those comfortable with disobedience.

**4** Ethical people link with other ethical people because iron sharpens iron. Unethical people link with other unethical people because there is no threat by truth to expose error.

**5** Never allow uninvited restless people to wander into your life.

**6** Those that do not build anything in your life, will eventually tear something down.

**7** Every person you become connected to, has other **Associations** in their life just like them.

---
D i a m o n d    W o r d s
---

*Blessed is the man that walketh not in the counsel of the ungodly, nor standeth in the way of sinners... Psalms 1:1*

# Attitude

**1** Your **Attitude** will determine your altitude.

**2** Excellence is the endeavor to be efficient, not the excuse to be arrogant.

**3** When you respond to ignorance, you perpetuate it.

**4** Never mistake success as the opportunity to be a snob.

**5** Your **Attitude** must say who you are, not who you are not.

**6** Treat everyone with respect.  You never know when the "errand boy" will become the "President"!

**7** What you display to others, will be what they believe about you.

---

### Diamond Words

*Let the words of my mouth, and the meditation of my heart, be acceptable in thy sight, O LORD, my strength, and my redeemer  Psalms 19:14*

# Belief Systems

**❶** Those that speak into your life, sculpture what you believe about it.

**❷** You will never change your life, until you change your **Belief System**.

**❸** A person's **Belief System** is what determines a person's Integrity System.

**❹** You will never change your **Belief System**, until you acknowledge that it is the reason for your present situations.

**❺** You only become vulnerable to information, when what you know cannot produce what you want.

**❻** The difference between success and failure, is in what you believe about it.

**❼** You will never "Raise Others," until you "Raise" what others think.

―――――― D i a m o n d     W o r d s ――――――

*A wise man will bear, and will increase learning; and a man of understanding shall attain unto wise counsels: Proverbs 1:5*

# Blessing

**1** A **Blessing** life will require a **Blessing** mentality.

**2** **Blessings** will often come from unpredictable sources, in unexplainable packages.

**3** **Blessings** will require you to look past the obvious, and see into the supernatural.

**4** **Blessings** are the proof of obedience.

**5** You must be as ruthless in protecting your **Blessings**, as you are in pursuing them.

**6** **Blessings** are motivated by Covenant Promise, not natural circumstance.

**7** **Blessings** can be scheduled into your life as easily as curses can.

---

### D i a m o n d    W o r d s

*And all these **Blessings** shall come on thee, and overtake thee, if thou shalt hearken unto the voice of the LORD thy God   Deuteronomy 28:2*

# Change

**1** Great leaders are quick to recognize error, and quicker to **Change** it.

**2** *God* will always **Change** you to greater, never average.

**3** *God* does not **Change** you to make you miserable, but to make you effective.

**4** In order to get to where you want to be, you must be willing to leave where you are at.

**5** *God* uses **Change** to clear your present canvas, so *He* can paint a future portrait.

**6** **Change** what you believe, in order to **Change** what you achieve.  **Change** the way you talk, in order to **Change** the steps you walk.  **Change** the seed you sow, in order to **Change** the harvest you grow.

**7** You will not succeed in your future, how you are in your present, so *God* makes **Changes** along the way.

--- D i a m o n d    W o r d s ---

*Being confident of this very thing, that he which hath begun a good work in you will perform it until the day of Jesus Christ   Philippians 1:6*

# Comfortability

**1** The *Holy Spirit* cannot lead you, anywhere you are not willing to go.

**2** The difference between coping and conquering is in how much you settle for.

**3** It only takes one mistake to expose how **Comfortable** you have become.

**4** Never become so **Comfortable** in what *God* has done, that you forget that *God* did it.

**5** Never become so **Comfortable** with where you are, that you make no plans to go further.

**6** When you are **Comfortable**, you are vulnerable.

**7** It's not until you get on the battlefield that you realize how relaxed you became in the palace.

---

**— D i a m o n d    W o r d s —**

*By much slothfulness the building decayeth; and through idleness of the hands the house droppeth through   Ecclesiastes 10:18*

# Communication

**1** Your words will either build a platform to stand on, or dig a ditch to fall in.

**2** Speak from your passion, not from someone else's.

**3** Words are the only opportunity you have to enter someone's moment, and change their lifetime.

**4** Say in a sentence, what others say in a paragraph.

**5** If you cannot arrive at the point, don't go on the journey.

**6** Allow your mind to load the gun, before you allow your mouth to pull the trigger.

**7** **Communication** is the ability to take people on a journey from where they are, to where they need to be.

---

### Diamond Words

*Let no corrupt **Communication** proceed out of your mouth, but that which is good to the use of edifying Ephesians 4:29*

# Communion

**1** Never run to the chaos of your conflict, before you run into the **Communion** of *"His Presence."*

**2** Make *His Presence* a habitation not a visitation.

**3** What you receive from *"His Presence,"* will be determined by how long you stay to get it.

**4** Once the staleness of ritual comes in, the spontaneity of relationship goes out.

**5** If *"His Presence"* does not "dominate your day," it will never "dominate your life."

**6** The more comfortable you become with *"His Presence,"* the more uncomfortable you will become with anything that disrupts it.

**7** The purpose of "time" in *"His Presence"* is to birth "intimacy." The purpose of "intimacy" is to birth "impartation."

───── D i a m o n d   W o r d s ─────

*The grace of the Lord Jesus Christ, and the love of God, and the **Communion** of the Holy Ghost, be with you all. Amen   II Corinthians 13:14*

# Confidence

**1** Let **Confidence** determine your steps, more than coincidence.

**2** **Confidence** is the only way others will know what you believe in.

**3** It matters not what others believe about you, as long as you believe in yourself.

**4** **Confidence** is an inward knowledge, not an outward arrogance.

**5** Quiet **Confidence** supersedes loud insecurity.

**6** **Confidence** never has to prove itself to intimidation.

**7** If you can believe in where you are going, then what you are facing cannot stop you from getting there.

---

D i a m o n d    W o r d s

*For the LORD shall be thy **Confidence**, and shall keep thy foot from being taken   Proverbs 3:26*

---

# Creativity

**1** Great leaders use their mind for **Creativity**, not memory.

**2** Great leaders look to desire for "Conception," and focus for "Completion."

**3** Be married to a result, not a method.

**4** **Creativity** Births.  Structure Completes.

**5** Your "Biggest Successes" are just a collection of "Small Adjustments."

**6** **Creativity** is an individuality, that similarity will never be.

**7** You will only maintain productivity, as long as you protect **Creativity**.

---
D i a m o n d     W o r d s
---

*...My heart is inditing a good matter: I speak of the things which I have made touching the king: my tongue is the pen of a ready writer.  Psalms 45:1*

# Criticism

**1** **Criticism** is just anothers way of envying your progress, and despising your difference.

**2** Often times when others **Criticize** you it's because they see in you the boldness to be a "stone," instead of the fear in themselves to just be a piece of the rock.

**3** Never defend your creativity to someone who is **Critical**.

**4** **Criticism** is a reaction of those who are intimidated in being "out done," more than motivated towards getting "more done."

**5** Champions strategize, losers **Criticize**.

**6** Those not making suggestions for your improvement, are unqualified to **Criticize** your achievements.

**7** **Criticism** will never destroy you, if it's not allowed to control you.

---
## D i a m o n d   W o r d s

*Having a good conscience; that, whereas they speak evil of you, as of evildoers, they may be ashamed that falsely accuse... I Peter 3:16*

# Debt

❶ **Debt** will put you in intentional situations, that blessings will have to bail you out of.

❷ **Debt** says you believe *God* to pay back more than to provide.

❸ **Debt** takes the right to exercise covenant promise out of *God's* hands.

❹ **Debt** makes you a prisoner to pressure, and a stranger to faith.

❺ **Debt** is not a sign of growth, it's a sign of doubt.

❻ Everything *God* has called you to do, *He* will pay for you to do it.

❼ Hate **Debt** as much as sin.

---

───── D i a m o n d    W o r d s ─────

*For the LORD thy God blesseth thee, as he promised thee: and thou shalt lend unto many nations, but thou shalt not borrow...*
*Deuteronomy 15:6*

# Decisions

**1** Your **Decisions** determine your circumstances. If you don't like your circumstances, change your **Decisions**.

**2** You will only make wrong **Decisions** from wrong information.

**3** "Pig Pens" are the result of a **Decision** to go somewhere *God* did not tell you to.

**4** You will never be more celebrated with "Right **Decisions**" and never more isolated with "Wrong Ones."

**5** Every **Decision** will either showcase your achievements, or your regrets.

**6** Today's **Decisions** determine tomorrow's provisions.

**7** Never be so loyal to a wrong **Decision**, that you refuse to let repentance reverse it.

—————— D i a m o n d     W o r d s ——————

*And thine ears shall hear a word behind thee, saying, This is the way, walk ye in it...*
*Isaiah 30:21*

# Depression

**1** The moment you stop moving toward something, **Depression** will make you a prisoner of nothing.

**2** **Depression** is the proof you have no photograph of a future.

**3** **Depression** is the devil's way of getting you one step closer to extinction.

**4** When vision walks out, **Depression** walks in.

**5** Misery is proof that what you're presently doing, is incapable of making you consistently happy.

**6** **Depression** is your enemies way of robbing your energy, by robbing your joy.

**7** You will only get **Depressed** at what you have, if you cannot see what *God* can do with it.

---

Diamond  Words

*Why art thou cast down, O my soul? and why art thou disquieted within me? hope thou in God: for I shall yet praise him, who is the health of my countenance, and my God   Psalms 42:11*

# Diligence

**1** **Diligence** to instruction increases responsibility.

**2** **Diligence** to detail increases dependability.

**3** **Diligence** to wisdom increases durability.

**4** **Diligence** to problem-solving increases reward-ability.

**5** **Diligence** to assignment increases achievability.

**6** **Diligence** to organization increases productivity.

**7** **Diligence** to focus removes instability.

---

D i a m o n d     W o r d s

*Seest thou a man **Diligent** in his business? he shall stand before kings; he shall not stand before mean men   Proverbs 22:29*

# Excellence

**①** **Excellence** will cost you what mediocrity will save you.

**②** **Excellent** people will conquer, what average people will complain about.

**③** **Excellent** people pursue solutions, average people stare at problems.

**④** **Excellence** orchestrates in your mind, translates in your speech, and demonstrates in your life.

**⑤** Others will notice your effort to be **Excellent**, more than your acceptance to be mediocre.

**⑥** Never expect someone else to tolerate the same lack of **Excellence,** that you would not.

**⑦** Make improvements, not excuses.

---

**Diamond    Words**

*In all things showing thyself a pattern of good works: in doctrine showing uncorruptness, gravity, sincerity   Titus 2:7*

# Failure

**❶** **Failure** is not final.  It's a temporary delay, not a permanent defeat.

**❷** **Failures** just expose what doesn't work, so you can focus your pursuit on what will.

**❸** The pain of **Failure** will stay with you, until the photograph of starting over supersedes it.

**❹** *God* uses the devastation of your setbacks, as the preparation for your comebacks.

**❺** Champions learn from defeat, losers live in it.

**❻** **Failure** is never possible, unless it's considered.

**❼** When man sees your **Failures**, he sees your end.  When *God* sees your **Failures**, *He* sees your beginning.

---

D i a m o n d    W o r d s

*Though he fall, he shall not be utterly cast down: for the LORD upholdeth him with his hand*
*Psalms 37:24*

# Faith

**1** **Faith** will make you believe with your spirit, what you cannot believe with your logic.

**2** **Faith** will require you to follow an instruction, without an explanation.

**3** When you can't believe in the problem, believe in the problem-solver.

**4** **Faith** is not the substitute for disobedience.

**5** It takes the same energy to believe, as it does to doubt.  However, the results are worlds apart.

**6** Believe in the compass of your heart.  It will guide you through the storms of inaccuracy, that your mind sometimes believes.

**7** **Faith** cannot launch its missiles, unless it sees the target.

---

**D i a m o n d     W o r d s**

*So then **Faith** cometh by hearing, and hearing by the word of God   Romans 10:17*

# Fatigue

**1** "Tired eyes" will never see "fresh vision."

**2** Achievement cannot justify burnout.

**3** If you can't "shut down," then you will "shut down."

**4** Schedule "refueling points" in your day.

**5** It's okay to work hard, as long as you rest "as hard."

**6** Your enemy will appear stronger, as you become weaker.

**7** If the "Presence of *God*" does not renew you, the "work of *God*" will not sustain you.

---

### Diamond Words

*And let us not be weary in well doing: for in due season we shall reap, if we faint not*
*Galatians 6:9*

# Favor

**1** **Favor** is the ability to get what you need, without having to do what you thought to get it.

**2** If you don't sow **Favor**, you won't reap it.

**3** The difference between where you are, and where you would like to be, is determined by somebody who can get you there.

**4** You cannot buy with money, what **Favor** can give to you.

**5** One person that celebrates you is worth more than a thousand people that tolerate you.

**6** Somebody is walking around with a blessing, and they are trying to find YOU!

**7** You are only one "Boaz" away from the barley fields to the palace.

---
### Diamond Words

*For thou, LORD, wilt bless the righteous; with **Favour** wilt thou compass him as with a shield    Psalms 5:12*

# Fears

◆1 Your assignment will reveal your **Fears**.

◆2 The only walls that stop you, will be the ones you build yourself.

◆3 You will never understand a person, until you understand a person's **Fears**.

◆4 **Fears** must be understood, before they can be overcome.

◆5 The more afraid you are to be yourself, the less afraid you'll be of being someone else.

◆6 If you never **Fear** what is on the other side of right, you will never maintain a fortress against what is wrong.

◆7 **FEAR**. False Evidence Appearing Real.

---
D i a m o n d      W o r d s
---

*For God hath not given us the spirit of fear; but of power, and of love, and of a sound mind. II Timothy 1:7*

# Focus

**1** You will never have a platform for your achievements, until you have a fortress around your **Focus**.

**2** If you can change your **Focus**, you can change your failure.

**3** Your **Focus** will offend those not permitted to distract it.

**4** If your enemy can have your **Focus**, he can have your life.

**5** No one else will guard your **Focus**, you will have to.

**6** If your enemy can keep your **Focus** on the land of problem, he can keep you out of the land of promise.

**7** Those who do not value your **Focus**, will not value your assignment either.

---
### ── D i a m o n d     W o r d s ──

*Looking unto Jesus the author and finisher of our faith; who for the joy that was set before him endured... Hebrews 12:2*

# Forgiveness

**1** It's not temporary offenses that kill you, but rather your permanent attachment to them that does.

**2** What you cannot release, you cannot restore.

**3** **Forgiveness** does not stop someone else from causing pain, it stops you from having to live with it.

**4** *God* **Forgives** you, so you can **Forgive** yourself.

**5** You cannot change what is in another person, you can only change what is in you.

**6** *God* does not measure **Forgiveness** according to the severity of your sin, but according to the transparency of your heart.

**7** **Forgiveness** begins with your ability to live honest, not your ability to live perfect.

---

D i a m o n d     W o r d s

*And be ye kind one to another, tenderhearted, **Forgiving** one another, even as God for Christ's sake hath **Forgiven** you   Ephesians 4:32*

# Future

**1** Your **Future** is a reward for being patient.

**2** Who you serve, determines who is capable of promoting you.

**3** Your heroes are a prophecy of your **Future**.

**4** If you have time to be lost, you have time to be defeated.

**5** One step in the right direction can erase all of your steps in the wrong one.

**6** The *Holy Spirit* cannot promote you, anywhere *He* cannot lead you.

**7** *God* uses "Temporary" seasons, to prepare you for "Permanent" ones.

---

D i a m o n d     W o r d s

*Commit thy way unto the LORD; trust also in him; and he shall bring it to pass. Psalms 37:5*

# Goals

**1** Be realistic. You can't achieve what you can't believe.

**2** Be married to the **Goal**, not the plan.

**3** Learn to eat a cow, a steak at a time.

**4** Build your team with completers, as well as thinkers.

**5** Always know where you are in proximity to achievement.

**6** If you don't have a **Goal**, you will never have a future.

**7** If you don't reach for something, you will settle for anything, and achieve nothing.

---

**D i a m o n d    W o r d s**

*For which of you, intending to build a tower, sitteth not down first, and counteth the cost, whether he have sufficient to finish it?*
*Luke 14:28*

---

# Habits

**1** Success and failure are separated by the kind of **Habits** you follow daily.

**2** Champions realize that their preparation determines their destination.

**3** **Habits** are forceful. The bad ones can hurt you, as much as the good ones can help you.

**4** You can only qualify a **Habit** by looking at the future it will produce.

**5** You cannot stop a wrong **Habit,** until you start a right one.

**6** It only requires a few "right things" in your day to make a lot of "right things" happen in your life.

**7** **Habits** are made to order. You must decide the ones that work best for you.

―――― D i a m o n d     W o r d s ――――

*So will I sing praise unto thy name for ever, that I may daily perform my vows  Psalms 61:8*

# Healing

**1** You have a right to anything you can believe for.

**2** The one who paid for your sickness, paid for your **Healing** at the same time.

**3** If sickness was the way *God* used to teach us a lesson, we'd have to stay in school all of the time.

**4** When you can let go of something *God* said *He* would carry, **Healing** can begin.

**5** **Healing** is *God's* way of always remaining a step ahead of logic.

**6** Just when you wonder if *God* can **Heal** you, *His* Word says *He* already has!

**7** As little doubt as it takes to stay sick, is as little faith as it takes to get well.

---

### Diamond Words

*But unto you that fear my name shall the Sun of righteousness arise with **Healing** in his wings; and ye shall go forth... Malachi 4:2*

# Health

❶ If **Health** does not matter to you, then healing is not your answer.

❷ A person that pursues **Health**, is a person who truly values what *God* has blessed them with.

❸ Healing is not a substitute for **Health**.

❹ How you protect *God's* blessing of "YOU," will determine how you will protect every other blessing *He* gives you.

❺ **Health** cannot be imparted, it must be pursued.

❻ Breakdown occurs when we attempt to get more out of our bodies, than we put in.

❼ **Health** decorates your appearance, and determines your endurance.

---

## Diamond Words

*Beloved, I wish above all things that thou mayest prosper and be in **Health**, even as thy soul prospereth   III John 1:2*

---

# Heroes

**1** Who you listen to, determines who you will follow.

**2** Who you look up to, determines who you will learn from.

**3** Who you defend, determines what you stand for.

**4** Who you value, determines who you will cover.

**5** Who you admire, determines who you will refer to.

**6** Who you respect, determines who has access to you.

**7** Who you celebrate, determines who you will imitate.

---

**D i a m o n d    W o r d s**

*...for the time would fail me to tell of Gedeon, and of Barak, and of Samson, and of Jephthae; of David also, and Samuel, and of the prophets: Who through faith subdued kingdoms, wrought righteousness, obtained promises, stopped the mouths of lions, Hebrews 11:32-33*

# Holiness

**1** The essence of **Holiness** is not in "Outward Appearance," but in "Inward Commitment."

**2** **Holiness** is how you are before *God*. How you are before *God*, will be how you are before people.

**3** **Holiness** begins with transparency, more than diplomacy before *God*.

**4** **Holiness** is found in those who "fear *God*," more than they patronize *Him*.

**5** If you are afraid of grieving *God*, then chances are you won't!

**6** If you fear grieving *God*, then you will fear grieving *God* in others.

**7** Sooner or later your actions will reveal the contents of your heart.

---

**————— D i a m o n d     W o r d s —————**

*And an highway shall be there, and a way, and it shall be called the way of **Holiness**; the unclean shall not pass over it   Isaiah 35:8*

---

# Holy Spirit

**1** Who *He* is matters more than what *He* does.

**2** The more of *Him* you acknowledge, the more of *Him* you access.

**3** The closer you come to *His* pleasures, the farther away you get from *His* griefs.

**4** When *He* is the priority, *He* will be the majority!

**5** Everything *God* promised that you could have, the **Holy Spirit** will lead you to it.

**6** *He* does not change in spite of your circumstances.

**7** When *He* moves, *He* moves as though the devil never existed.

---

**D i a m o n d  W o r d s**

*And I will pray the Father, and he shall give you another Comforter, that he may abide with you for ever  John 14:16*

---

# Hope

**1** Hope is *God's* permission to go after everything *He* said you could have.

**2** **Hope** sees the possible of tomorrow, passed the impossible of today.

**3** **Hope** is the affirmation that lets you know you can have what you see.

**4** When **Hope** is gone, so is the ability to see your future different from your past.

**5** **Hope** is the proof you don't have to stay where you are.

**6** If you can't believe in yourself, you won't believe in your future.

**7** When your circumstances offer no **Hope**, the *God* of your circumstances does.

---

———— D i a m o n d    W o r d s ————

*Be of good courage, and he shall strengthen your heart, all ye that **Hope** in the LORD*
*Psalms 31:24*

# Hospitality

**1** **Hospitality** is a seed *God* allows you to sow, to permit others to sow it into you.

**2** **Hospitality** disarms hostility.

**3** Blessings are the proof, *God* has made it possible for you to be good to somebody.

**4** Those who serve, are remembered as much as those who lead.

**5** Excellence is impossible without **Hospitality**.

**6** **Hospitality** is proof you despise greed.

**7** **Hospitality** says anothers comfort matters to you as much as your own.

---

### Diamond Words

*That they do good, that they be rich in good works, ready to distribute, willing to communicate   I Timothy 6:18*

---

# Individuality

① Celebrate what makes you an **Individual**, not a copy.

② If you don't give away who you are, you will never become someone you are not.

③ Comparisons to others are sometimes complimentary. However, oftentimes it's merely someone else's attempt to categorize your **Individuality**, because of a lack of their own.

④ Others will never mimic a copy, only an original.

⑤ Always be a person, not a possession.

⑥ The sale of your independence, is the last stage before obscurity.

⑦ Confident people know who they are, the insecure prove who they are.

---

——— D i a m o n d     W o r d s ———
*I will praise thee; for I am fearfully and wonderfully made   Psalms 139:14*

---

# Information

**❶** **Information** narrows the gap between where you are, and where you want to be.

**❷** Always obtain enough **Information** to make a qualified decision.

**❸** The kind of **Information** you lack, is contained in the kind of questions you ask.

**❹** Never try to use partial **Information** to make a whole point.

**❺** Make **Information** accessible. What you can't find, you can't use.

**❻** The wise identify what they lack, and go after those who possess it.

**❼** You are always one piece of **Information** away from a breakthrough.

---

**D i a m o n d     W o r d s**

*The entrance of thy words giveth light; it giveth understanding unto the simple*
*Psalms 119:130*

# Instruction

**1** If you cannot obey an **Instruction**, having a destination won't help you.

**2** You will always get more **Instructions**, before you get more blessings.

**3** Every time the *Holy Spirit* gives you an **Instruction**, *He* has already walked to the other side of it, and seen the eventuality of your obedience.

**4** The bridge between where you are, and where you want to be, will be built by acts of obedience.

**5** The *Holy Spirit* will never give you an **Instruction** to consider, *He* will give you an **Instruction** to follow.

**6** You are never qualified for a new **Instruction**, until you have obeyed a present one.

**7** Every time you ignore an **Instruction**, you abort a miracle.

---
D i a m o n d     W o r d s
---

*...if thou shalt hearken diligently unto the voice of the LORD thy God, to observe and to do all his commandments... Deuteronomy 28:1*

# Integrity

**1** **Integrity** does not increase your calling, it increases your character.

**2** **Integrity** is practiced, diplomacy is proclaimed.

**3** **Integrity** is birthed by the wrong you have caused others, and sculptured by the wrong others have caused you.

**4** Real **Integrity** will birth in you a hatred for false pretenses.

**5** **Integrity** will only develop in you, when the pain of your mistakes births enough conviction to silence repetition.

**6** Connect with those who "sharpen your **Integrity**," not soothe your lack of it.

**7** The more that **Integrity** flows through you, the more unethical people will be uncomfortable around you.

───── D i a m o n d    W o r d s ─────

*The just man walketh in his **Integrity**: his children are blessed after him   Proverbs 20:7*

# Jealousy

**1** Those who criticize where you're going, are those incapable of giving you what you're going after.

**2** **Jealousy** is not motivated by who you are, but by where you are at.

**3** Champions are motivated by what losers are intimidated by.

**4** Manipulating leaders are really just insecure followers, with a **Jealousy** problem.

**5** **Jealous** people are those who have become more side tracked by where you are, instead of where they could be.

**6** Those that do not value your assignment, will never value your achievements.

**7** Never defend what you see, to those who don't see it.

───── D i a m o n d     W o r d s ─────
*For **Jealousy** is the rage of a man: therefore he will not spare in the day of vengeance.*
**Proverbs 6:34**

# Joy

1. Misery is simply the indicator you are looking at the wrong source to bring you **Joy**.

2. **Joy** has nothing to do with success.

3. If you cannot **Enjoy** the *Holy Spirit*, you will never **Enjoy** life.

4. You will never **Enjoy** anything *God* does not give you.

5. **Joy** is anywhere *"His Presence"* is.

6. You will never **Enjoy** another person that does not extract **Joy**, from the same *Holy Spirit* that you do.

7. If the *Holy Spirit* is not the center of your day, *His* **Joy** will never be the fruit of your life.

---

────── D i a m o n d   W o r d s ──────

*Thou wilt show me the path of life: in thy presence is fulness of **Joy**; at thy right hand there are pleasures for evermore   Psalms 16:11*

# Knowledge

**1** Warfare does not begin when you feel something, it begins when you learn something.

**2** It's not who you are that intimidates your enemy, it's what you know about who you are that does.

**3** **Knowledge** slams the door of deception that your enemy has come in and out of, to defeat you.

**4** **Knowledge** is only for those not satisfied with just the euphoria of feeling.

**5** When you move with what you know, God teaches you what you don't.

**6** **Knowledge** is for the hungry, not the haughty.

**7** Increase cannot be expected, unless **Knowledge** is pursued.

---
D i a m o n d    W o r d s
---

*My people are destroyed for lack of*
***Knowledge...*** *Hosea 4:6*

# Leadership

**1** **Leadership** is the ability to lead somebody where you have been, rather than order them to go somewhere you have not.

**2** **Leaders** build memorials rather than create casualties.

**3** **Leadership** is the ability to motivate others to follow you, instead of force them to come.

**4** **Leaders** prepare others for their future, rather than possess others in their present.

**5** **Leaders** are former followers who mastered focus and conquered pride.

**6** **Leadership** is the ability to motivate everybody to do something, instead of somebody to do everything.

**7** **Leaders** learn from mistakes, followers live with them.

---

————— D i a m o n d      W o r d s —————

*And the things that thou hast heard of me among many witnesses, the same commit thou to faithful men, who shall be able to teach others also   II Timothy 2:2*

# Legacies

**1** Multiplication is the greatest reward.

**2** Your life will only be known by the **Legacy** you leave.

**3** A successor is proof *God* did not intend for your mantle to die, when you do.

**4** Wise mentors prepare more for their future, than live for their present.

**5** Your life is a classroom for the next generation.

**6** What you build for yourself, will die when you do.

**7** Achievers see yesterday's heroes as today's teachers.

---

**D i a m o n d     W o r d s**

*When I call to remembrance the unfeigned faith that is in thee, which dwelt first in thy grandmother Lois, and thy mother Eunice; and I am persuaded that in thee also.  II Timothy 1:5*

# Loyalty

**❶** **Loyalty** is a gift you cannot buy from another, or sell yourself.

**❷** **Loyalty** is not what you promise, it's what you practice.

**❸** Reward **Loyalty**.  If it doesn't become important, it may become absent.

**❹** Those that do not guard others, will not guard you.

**❺** Stand behind your word, not away from it.

**❻** A person's motives will answer the questions for their existence.

**❼** The moment you can purchase **Loyalty**, is the moment it can be sold for a higher price.

---

——— D i a m o n d    W o r d s ———
*Faithful are the wounds of a friend; but the kisses of an enemy are deceitful   Proverbs 27:6*

# Mentorship

**1** A **Mentor** is *God's* guarantee that your future will not be the same as your past.

**2** You do not decide who you will connect to, you discover whom *God* is linking you to.

**3** If somebody does not change from being in your life, then that is proof they did not come into your life to change.

**4** The rewards of your achievements will be accompanied by the responsibility to teach others to achieve.

**5** Proof of the kind of future *God* has assigned for you is determined by the kind of **Mentor** *He* connects you to.

**6** A **Mentor** already knows what he/she can do for the protégé, but it's not until the protege realizes what the **Mentor** can do, that the benefits of connection begin.

**7** A **Mentor** is proof that *God* thought enough of your assignment, that *He* gave you someone to help you achieve it.

---

### Diamond Words

*And Joshua the son of Nun was full of the spirit of wisdom; for Moses had laid his hands upon him...Deuteronomy 34:9*

# Ministry

1. The success of **Ministry** is determined by what others are able to do, as a result of something you have done for them.

2. Success is not in numbers, it is in effectiveness.

3. Who you are with *God* privately, will be what you are for *God* publicly.

4. Let your prayer life be the reason for your **Ministry**, instead of your **Ministry** be the reason for your prayer life.

5. You will never successfully help others until you identify the problems *God* has assigned you to solve, and the people who have them.

6. If the *God* of **Ministry** can dominate you, then the machinery of **Ministry** will not control you.

7. If you don't fail *God*, you won't fail *God's* people.

---
D i a m o n d　　W o r d s
---

*If thou put the brethren in remembrance of these things, thou shalt be a good minister of Jesus Christ... I Timothy 4:6*

# Miracles

**1** **Miracles** are *God's* greatest incentive to force us towards *His* greatest pleasure...believing *Him.*

**2** You will only experience the **Miraculous**, when the passion of pursuit overwhelms the plague of passivity.

**3** You cannot access your **Miracle**, until you address your need.

**4** *God* is more excited to show you the **Miraculous**, than you are to see it.

**5** It takes the same amount of faith to accept defeat, as it does to expect victory.

**6** No one else has to believe in your **Miracle**, only you!

**7** You are only one **Miracle** away from a turn-around.

---

### Diamond Words

*Ye men of Israel, hear these words; Jesus of Nazareth, a man approved of God among you by **Miracles** and wonders and signs...   Acts 2:22*

# Misery

**❶ Misery** is the proof you are looking at the wrong sources to bring you joy.

**❷ Misery** is the proof your focus is on something that is draining you, rather than sustaining you.

**❸ Misery** is the proof you are exhausting too much energy, trying to go somewhere the *Holy Spirit* is not leading you.

**❹ Misery** is the proof you are spending too much time fighting battles that *God* said *He* would fight for you.

**❺ Misery** is the proof you are spending too much time pursuing something the *Holy Spirit* is not giving you.

**❻ Misery** is the proof you are making unnecessary demands on people to satisfy you.

**❼ Misery** is the proof that you think achievements are a relevant substitution for relationship with the *Holy Spirit.*

---

Diamond    Words

*Then I will go back to my place until they admit their guilt. And they will seek my face; in their **Misery**...   Hosea 5:15 (NIV)*

---

# Money

1. What you love, will come towards you.

2. Never sacrifice your future, to create your present.

3. How do you assassinate greed?  Do something a greedy person would not do...give.

4. Your assignment is just a thought, until **Money** makes it a reality.

5. When you complain about your seed, you corrupt your harvest.

6. The wealthy understand that nothing is ever multiplied, unless it is managed.

7. **Money** is a reward for solving problems. (Mike Murdock)

---
## Diamond Words

*For wisdom is a defence, and **Money** is a defence: but the excellency of knowledge is, that wisdom giveth life to them that have it.*
*Ecclesiastes 7:12*

---

# Motivation

**1** Improvements are only as quick, as your **Motivation** to correct deficiency.

**2** Inferiority that is **Motivated**, will go further than superiority that is complacent.

**3** Complacency never starts "big." It begins "small" and gains momentum.

**4** The brick wall is not a sign your enemy has stopped you, it is a sign you have not found the door yet.

**5** **Motivation** is what destroys complacency, and determines tenacity.

**6** You will never be **Motivated** by anothers vision, unless it's your vision.

**7** Move towards those who "energize where you are going," more than "sympathize with where you have come from."

——— D i a m o n d     W o r d s ———

*Be strong and of a good courage...for the LORD thy God, he it is that doth go with thee; he will not fail thee, nor forsake thee   Deuteronomy 31:6*

# Movement

**1** Never stop the **Movement** towards your future, by "Self Defending" your present.

**2** Champions pursue, what losers wait for.

**3** Giving Begins Something.  Greed Concludes it.

**4** When you want something to react towards you, take a step towards it.

**5** Great leaders never defend their **Movement** to pessimistic followers.

**6** Never stop your **Movement** for retaliation.

**7** The difference between "Waiting" and "Pursuing" is information.

---

D  i  a  m  o  n  d     W  o  r  d  s

*For in him we live, and move, and have our being; as certain also of your own poets have said, For we are also his offspring.  Acts 17:28*

# Never

**❶ Never** believe everyone else is blind.

**❷ Never** brag about something, your conduct cannot back up.

**❸ Never** promise something reality cannot produce.

**❹ Never** distort truth to gain favor.

**❺ Never** gossip to gain acceptance.

**❻ Never** believe the lie, "I won't get caught."

**❼ Never** be afraid to acknowledge, "I missed it."

---

**D i a m o n d    W o r d s**

*And an angel of the LORD came up...and said, I made you to go up out of Egypt, and have brought you unto the land which I sware unto your fathers; and I said, I will **Never** break my covenant with you. Judges 2:1*

# Obedience

1. **Obedience** is the only way *God* can guarantee your outcome.

2. You have a right to everything you have **Obeyed**.

3. Permanent devastation can take place in temporary **Disobedience**.

4. **Disobedience** will be the springboard for unnecessary demonic warfare in your life.

5. *God* will not get involved with **Disobedience**, except through repentance.

6. **Disobedience** will prove the futility of doing things your way.

7. **Obedience** is an action, not a confession.

---

—— D i a m o n d    W o r d s ——
*If ye be willing and **Obedient**, ye shall eat the good of the land    Isaiah 1:19*

# Observation

◆ **Observation** will reveal what education cannot.

◆ **Observe** how great people handle great adversity.

◆ Whatever you can **Observe**, you can understand. Whatever you can understand you can master.

◆ If you can **Observe** your environment, you can position yourself to handle it.

◆ Discernment is the *Holy Spirit's* way to allow you to see things as they really are, instead of how they appear to be.

◆ You can't stop the flood, until you can **Observe** the leak.

◆ Watch when others don't think you're watching. Listen when others don't think you're listening.

─────── D i a m o n d    W o r d s ───────

*For Herod feared John, knowing that he was a just man and an holy, and **Observed** him; and when he heard him, he did many things, and heard him gladly   Mark 6:20*

# Organization

**1** The longer you live with disorder, the longer you will live with the pain it produces.

**2** When something is in the right place, it can produce the right results.

**3** **Organization** will never begin, until the pain of clutter becomes too overwhelming.

**4** **Organize** your structure around what works best for who you are, and where you are at.

**5** If people don't know their position, they will never know their purpose.

**6** **Organize** your goals with an ending, not just a beginning.

**7** The first step towards **Organization**, is the honesty to admit something is out of place.

---
— D i a m o n d    W o r d s —

*For God is not the author of confusion, but of peace, as in all churches of the saints*
*I Corinthians 14:33*

---

# Pain

**1** **Pain** is the motivator for change, that pleasure will never be.

**2** Expose Hurt.  Maintaining it makes it grow, releasing it makes it die.

**3** When you rehearse past mistakes, you prepare yourself to repeat them.

**4** You must agree to leave your past, before *God* can agree to start your future.

**5** **Pain** is only present when it is protected.

**6** You must interrogate the reasons why something has hurt you, before you can calculate a proper response to it.

**7** If **Pain** was never real, the ability to help others through it would not be possible.

---

D i a m o n d    W o r d s

*He healeth the broken in heart, and bindeth up their wounds   Psalms 147:3*

# Past

1. Redemption is *God's* way of staying one step ahead of religion.

2. Those that refuse to leave their **Past**, are addicted to the attention that re-living it produces.

3. When you look behind, you fall behind.

4. The reason *God* does not visit your **Past**, is because *He* refuses to focus on something *He* is incapable of changing.

5. Champions learn from their **Past**, losers live in it.

6. When you rehearse **Past** memories, you relive **Past** pain.

7. Your enemy uses your **Past** for "Condemnation," *God* uses your past for "Revelation."

---

D i a m o n d     W o r d s

*Brethren, I count not myself to have apprehended: but this one thing I do, forgetting those things which are behind, and reaching forth unto those things which are before, Philippians 3:13*

# Patience

**1** The purpose of the *Holy Spirit's* leading, is to birth the "conviction of **Patience**" in you, so your enemy will be unable to use the "weapon of **Impatience**" to sabotage your destiny.

**2** **Impatience** will rob time of being your ally.

**3** The only way *God's* purpose can come to pass, is if *God's* timing brings it.

**4** Most equate **Patience** with passivity. *God* equates it with trust.

**5** **Patience** will offend those not allowed to manipulate you with haste.

**6** **Patience** will keep you out of the "pit" of presumption.

**7** **Patience** disarms your enemies' strategy to abort the entry of something *God* has already scheduled into your future.

─────── D i a m o n d    W o r d s ───────

*But let **Patience** have her perfect work, that ye may be perfect and entire, wanting nothing*
*James 1:4*

# People

**1** **People** are *God's* way of "blessing" you, and the enemy's way of "stressing" you.

**2** **People** are *God's* way of helping you over, and the enemy's way of keeping you under.

**3** **People** are *God's* way of adding to your assignment, and the enemy's way of distracting it.

**4** **People** are *God's* way of supporting your strengths, and the enemy's way of distorting your weaknesses.

**5** **People** are *God's* link to your future, and your enemy's link to your past.

**6** If a person's words cannot survive interrogation, they are unqualified for consideration.

**7** Never reach for those not reaching.

---
— D i a m o n d    W o r d s —

*He that walketh with wise men shall be wise: but a companion of fools shall be destroyed*
*Proverbs 13:20*

# Pleasure

**1** **Pleasure** will never be present until it is scheduled.

**2** **Pleasure** is the ability to enjoy something you love.

**3** **Pleasure** will never be plentiful, until it is pursued.

**4** Schedule enough **Pleasure**, that regret has no room for accusation.

**5** Be good to yourself.  How good you are to you, determines how good you are to others.

**6** Learn to disconnect.  You can't clear your problems, until you can clear your mind.

**7** Make appointments to play, just like you make them to work.

---
D i a m o n d     W o r d s
---

*...Let the LORD be magnified, which hath* ***Pleasure*** *in the prosperity of his servant* *Psalms 35:27*

# Prayer

**1** Results are not the reason you **Pray**, they are the proof that you do.

**2** **Prayer** is a place where you bond with your "Best Friend," the *Holy Spirit.*

**3** You will never enjoy **Prayer**, if you do not enjoy *"His Presence."*

**4** When who you are **Praying** to, becomes more important than what you are **Praying** for, what you are **Praying** for will change from a need to an answer.

**5** When the "desire" for *God* is birthed, the discipline to spend time with *God* will emerge.

**6** The purpose of **Prayer** is not to secure possessions, it is to receive impartation.

**7** Five minutes of relationship, is worth more than five hours of ritual.

—— D i a m o n d      W o r d s ——

*If my people, which are called by my name, shall humble themselves, and **Pray**...*
*II Chronicles 7:14*

# Preparation

**1)** If you don't **Prepare** to succeed, you will prepare to fail.

**2)** The absence of **Preparation** will bring the presence of devastation.

**3)** *God* can change your direction, but you must **Prepare** to go somewhere first.

**4)** You will never reach completion unless you have **Prepared** a map to the finish line.

**5)** Write your plans. You cannot run with a thought.

**6)** **Preparation** says that you are planning to succeed in what you are doing.

**7)** **Prepare** with what you have. Have faith for what you don't, and you will achieve what you could not.

───── D i a m o n d     W o r d s ─────

*The **Preparations** of the heart in man, and the answer of the tongue, is from the LORD*
*Proverbs 16:1*

# Present

❶ Today is the photograph of tomorrow. If you are going to change tomorrow, you must change today.

❷ Extract enough from where you are, that you can "Multiply" where you are going.

❸ Be a voice for something, instead of silent for everything.

❹ You will always speak out of your **Present** season.

❺ Do not look so far into the future, that you overlook those who got you to your **Present**.

❻ Your **Present** will either be a progression of your past, or a propeller of your future.

❼ Lethargy will detain you past the expiration date of your **Present** season.

---
────── D i a m o n d      W o r d s ──────

*For I reckon that the sufferings of this **Present** time are not worthy to be compared with the glory which shall be revealed in us.   Romans 8:18*

# Pressure

**1** **Pressure** is the proof you are spending your life trying to live up to another's standards.

**2** *God's* instructions will produce faith, your ideas will produce **Pressure**.

**3** Wise counsel relieves the **Pressure** of wrong decisions.

**4** **Pressure** is magnified when facilitating a wrong idea.

**5** Stress is the proof you are not doing things *God's* way.

**6** **Pressure** will only be as big as what you decide to tolerate.

**7** If you walk in character, you will never be under **Pressure** of trying to hide your actions.

---
## D i a m o n d    W o r d s

*It is vain for you to rise up early, to sit up late, to eat the bread of sorrows: for so he giveth his beloved sleep   Psalms 127:2*

# Pride

**1** Success will never build a high enough tower, that **Pride** cannot knock down.

**2** **Pride** will keep you in a state of denial, that change has no access to.

**3** **Pride** will build a fortress around error, that truth has no access to.

**4** **Pride** is never more reasonable than in the "Palace," and never more regretful than in the "Pig Pen."

**5** Humility is the access door to information, **Pride** is the enemy that shuts it.

**6** Never think of something you have done, as the greatest it will ever be.

**7** Keep enough **Pride** about yourself, to maintain a momentum of improvement.

---
D i a m o n d   W o r d s
---

*The fear of the LORD is to hate evil: **Pride**, and arrogancy, and the evil way, and the froward mouth, do I hate.  Proverbs 8:13*

# Problem–Solving

**1)** Never complain about anything you won't attempt to solve.

**2)** Average people point out problems, excellent people solve them.

**3)** Those that never get involved, never get promoted.

**4)** Those who do not solve problems, start them.

**5)** **Problem-Solving** is determined by the willingness to react, more than the carelessness to observe.

**6)** Problems you are incapable of solving, will not stand out to you.

**7)** Diplomacy is the harbor through the storms of commitment.

---

*Diamond Words*

*Without counsel purposes are disappointed: but in the multitude of counsellors they are established   Proverbs 15:22*

---

# Pursuit

**1** Never ask *God* to give you something, you are unwilling to go after.

**2** You will never possess something until the **Pursuit** of going after it, overwhelms the passivity of living without it.

**3** Present **Pursuit**, will require you to move through memories of past failures.

**4** **Pursuit** will require you to take a step with nothing.

**5** **Pursuit** begins with your desire, not anothers permission.

**6** **Pursuit** silences regret from creating photographs of what you could have had, had you **Pursued**.

**7** When you want something you have never had, you have got to do something you have never done.  (Dr. Mike Murdock)

—————— D i a m o n d   W o r d s ——————

*For every one that asketh receiveth; and he that seeketh findeth; and to him that knocketh it shall be opened   Matthew 7:8*

# Questions

**1** **Questions** reveal the humility to acknowledge something you don't know, and the hunger to find it.

**2** Those who never ask, never learn.

**3** You must identify the information you need, before you can qualify the **Questions** to get it.

**4** Those who never interrogate greatness, never become great.

**5** Specific information can only be accessed by specific **Questions**.

**6** Intimate information, can only be accessed by considerate **Questions.**

**7** Those that hate interrogation, hate information.

---

**————— D i a m o n d    W o r d s —————**

*If any of you lack wisdom, let him ask of God, that giveth to all men liberally, and upbraideth not; and it shall be given him.*
*James 1:5*

# Reactions

**1** Great leaders never answer something that has not been asked.

**2** The "High Road" will require as much humility, as integrity.

**3** One right **Reaction**, can position you for a lot of right favor.

**4** Wrong does not require two people.

**5** Anothers leverage against you, is based on how they think you will react.

**6** Don't analyze what you don't see, don't criticize what you don't understand.

**7** Right **Reactions** are the proof you have learned from the wrong ones.

---

D i a m o n d    W o r d s

*He that answereth a matter before he heareth it, it is folly and shame unto him.  Proverbs 18:13*

# Relationship

**1** When *God* wants to birth a future, *He* births a **Relationship**. When the enemy wants to destroy a future, he births a **Relationship**.

**2** Unnecessary **Relationships** produce unrealistic expectations.

**3** Opposition is never present until multiplication is possible.

**4** You will be known as much for the people you avoid, as much as the ones you associate with.

**5** Never attempt to take people past the "expiration date" of their seasons in your life.

**6** Celebrate the "Seasons" *God* puts people in your life, and the "Reasons" *He* takes them out.

**7** Don't be a "pack rat" of wrong people.

---
D i a m o n d     W o r d s
---

*Be ye not unequally yoked together with unbelievers: for what fellowship hath righteousness with unrighteousness?...  II Corinthians 6:14*

# Resources

**1** You will never reach for the expertise of others, until you acknowledge your own weakness.

**2** The sacrifice of something you want, will determine the possession of something you want more.

**3** Never ask directions, from someone who does not understand where you are going.

**4** The life long "School of Wisdom" has varied teachers. Dip your pail in the wells of many.

**5** Those you become linked to, are those you will imitate.

**6** The moment you invite corrupt individuals into your assignment, is the moment you invite their tragedy to sabotage it.

**7** If you could succeed alone, you would have already reached the top!

---

### Diamond Words

*Go to the ant, thou sluggard; consider her ways, and be wise: Which having no guide, overseer, or ruler, Provideth her meat in the summer, and gathereth her food in the harvest. Proverbs 6:6-8*

# Restlessness

**1** **Restlessness** is the enemy of faith, to keep you from waiting for something *God* promised to give you.

**2** **Restlessness** magnifies the pitfalls of options.

**3** **Restlessness** will lead you on a hunt for unnecessary things.

**4** **Restlessness** will cost you, what waiting will save you.

**5** **Restlessness** will use the motivation of curiosity to lead your steps towards the destruction of an enemy trap.

**6** **Restlessness** will make you search in wrong places, where wrong people hang out.

**7** **Restlessness** will take you on a journey that the *Holy Spirit* will not accompany you on.

─────── D i a m o n d   W o r d s ───────

*Be still, and know that I am God: I will be exalted among the heathen, I will be exalted in the earth   Psalms 46:10*

# Restoration

**1** **Restoration** works according to *God's* purpose, not man's permission.

**2** **Restoration** to *God's* purpose, begins with isolation in *God's* presence.

**3** *God* will use the devastation of your setbacks, as the platform for your comebacks.

**4** The past is last behind the front runner of a new beginning.

**5** Man can predict your outcome, only *God* can determine it.

**6** **Restoration** is the journey towards your future, not the jail house for your present.

**7** Those who have never been through the fire, are incapable of walking you through it.

---
**——— D i a m o n d     W o r d s ———**

*For your shame ye shall have double; and for confusion they shall rejoice in their portion*
*Isaiah 61:7*

---

79

# Schedule

**1** If you don't plan your **Schedule**, you will be dominated by someone else's.

**2** Those that will distract your **Schedule**, are those that do not have one themselves.

**3** **Schedule** something daily that you love to do, as much as you **Schedule** something daily that you have to do.

**4** If you do not value time, you will never value your assignment.

**5** Unless you value your own **Schedule**, you will never be considerate of someone else's.

**6** **Schedule** the exit of something, at the same time you **Schedule** the entrance.

**7** When you document your day, you determine the strategies for tomorrow.

---

D i a m o n d    W o r d s

*Redeeming the time, because the days are evil*
*Ephesians 5:16*

---

# Sin

**1** You were called to forsake **Sin**, not handle it.

**2** **Sinful** acts happen in **Sinful** situations.

**3** Grace is not an excuse to **Sin**, it's a harbor when you do.

**4** **Sin** does not come in different sizes.

**5** **Sin** is a deception, not a disease.

**6** **Sin** will not kill you, as much as your efforts to hide it will.

**7** If you expose temptation, you will expel devastation.

---

D i a m o n d     W o r d s

*For **Sin** shall not have dominion over you: for ye are not under the law, but under grace*
*Romans 6:14*

# Sowing

**1** **Seed** allows heaven's miracles to be earth's reality.

**2** Your harvest will only be as consistent as your **Seed**.

**3** **Sowing** is your only way of using your present to create your future.

**4** The only reason *God* will tell you to **Sow**, is because what you have, is not enough to be what you need.

**5** Before *God* ever tells you to **Sow** a **Seed**, *He* has already seen the harvest it will produce.

**6** Every **Seed** you **Sow** becomes a memorial of your faith, and a burial of your greed.

**7** When something leaves your present, it goes into your future, and prepares your future for your arrival there.

---

D i a m o n d  W o r d s

*Give, and it shall be given unto you; good measure, pressed down, and shaken together, and running over... Luke 6:38*

---

# Strength

**1** **Strength** is determined by focus. What you look at either motivates you, or stagnates you.

**2** Never use the **Strength** for achieving your goal, convincing others to believe in it.

**3** Disconnect from those who "sympathize" where you are at, and move towards those who "energize" where you are going.

**4** You will use more **Strength** pursuing an option, than you will following an instruction.

**5** What you have a "love for," you will have a "longevity in."

**6** **Strength** must be "daily renewed," or it will be "eventually expired."

**7** The strategy to replace a mistake, comes from the honesty to admit you made one.

---

Diamond    Words

*But they that wait upon the LORD shall renew their **Strength**; they shall mount up with wings as eagles; they shall run, and not be weary; and they shall walk, and not faint    Isaiah 40:31*

# Stress

**1** **Stress** magnifies when you're not in the "Center of your Expertise."

**2** Disobedience produces need.

**3** **Stressful** decisions produce **Stressful** conditions.

**4** Unrealistic focus, produces unnecessary **Stress**.

**5** **Stress** never changes, until your tolerance level for it does.

**6** **Stress** is not the presence of adversity, it's the absence of direction.

**7** For every day you're not soaring in the "Secret Place," you're surviving in the "**Stress** Place."

---

D i a m o n d    W o r d s

*Better is a dry morsel, and quietness therewith, than an house full of sacrifices with strife.*
*Proverbs 17:1*

# Success

**1** **Success** is not immunity from adversity, it's just the proof you conquered it.

**2** **Success** is a reward for staying focused.

**3** **Successful** people are just former failures who changed their focus.

**4** Savor your **Successes**.  You will always have time to ponder your mistakes.

**5** You will only keep your **Successes** as long as you keep your focus.

**6** **Success** is not measured in the size of your assignment, it's measured in the "obedience to your assignment."

**7** The difference between **Success** and failure is what you master.

——————— D i a m o n d     W o r d s ———————

*This book of the law shall not depart out of thy mouth; but thou shalt meditate therein day and night,...and then thou shalt have good success  Joshua 1:8*

# Talent

**1** Opportunity will expose your **Talents**. Opposition will expand them.

**2** *God* may change who you are, but *He* will never change what *He* made you.

**3** When you discover your "assignment," you will discover your **Talent**.

**4** Your **Talent** will never be used, if you are always comparing it to someone else's.

**5** **Talent** does not make you different. Assignment makes you different. **Talent** makes your assignment possible.

**6** Never underestimate *God's* ability to use "short term" **Talents**, to create "long term" dividends.

**7** "Right focus" will refine "raw **Talent**."

---

Diamond    Words

*I can do all things through Christ which strengtheneth me   Philippians 4:13*

---

# Thanksgiving

**1** Gratitude expands your boundaries for blessing.

**2** Gratitude releases others to be generous to you.

**3** Reward those who helped you, that did not have to.

**4** Go the extra mile to reward those that went the extra mile.

**5** **"Thank You"** is the ageless term, with "Endless Rewards."

**6** When you're **Thankful**, you're teachable.

**7** People are touched by gratitude, more than they are impressed with aptitude.

---

D i a m o n d   W o r d s

*Let us come before his presence with*
***Thanksgiving****, and make a joyful noise*
*unto him with psalms   Psalms 95:2*

---

# Thoughts

**1** **Thoughts** are a prelude to action. What you meditate on will be what you take a step towards.

**2** The longer you keep wrong **Thoughts** in your mind, the closer you will come to having wrong acts in your life.

**3** The kinds of **Thoughts** your enemy will seed your mind with, are linked to the kinds of areas he has planned for your failure in.

**4** If you can change your **Thoughts**, you can change your future.

**5** Failure is never evident until it is **Thought** about.

**6** When you keep wrong memories in your mind, you keep wrong people in your life.

**7** **Thinking** is the prelude to becoming.

---

——— D i a m o n d    W o r d s ———

*For as he **Thinketh** in his heart, so is he: Eat and drink, saith he to thee; but his heart is not with thee   Proverbs 23:7*

# Time

**1** **Time** interrogates others people's promises, until believability emerges.

**2** **Time** allows revelation to repair your failures.

**3** **Time** keeps you where you are, long enough for *God* to supply the resources to stay, or the instructions to leave.

**4** **Time** is a universal currency. What you purchase with it will determine your future.

**5** **Time** is a precious treasure, that is why your enemy keeps trying to steal yours.

**6** **Time** interrogates possibility, until direction emerges.

**7** **Time** keeps you in your present season, long enough to become over qualified for it.

---

D i a m o n d    W o r d s

*To every thing there is a season, and a **Time** to every purpose under the heaven: Ecclesiastes 3:1*

# Tragedy

**1** If you wait to release a **Tragedy** until you can explain it, you will place your recovery on indefinite delay.

**2** If you never get over the reasons of why you fell down, you will never grasp the reasons for why you should get back up.

**3** Champions move beyond, where losers choose to stay.

**4** Those that can survive a crash, are greater than those that think they never will.

**5** *God* can enter through the "trap door" of a mistake, and lead you to the place *He* was unable to lead you prior to that point.

**6** If your desire does not move you towards *God*, your calamity will.

**7** When you have nothing left but *God*, you have got enough to start again (Mike Murdock).

---
### Diamond Words
*...Give unto them beauty for ashes, the oil of joy for mourning, the garment of praise for the spirit of heaviness...   Isaiah 61:3*

# Truth

**1** **Truth** is never evident until it's applied.

**2** Those who embrace **Truth**, have no tolerance for those who embrace error.

**3** Those who embrace **Truth**, will risk correction in order to find it.

**4** You will never arrive at **Truth**, until you go on an "Unbias" journey to find it.

**5** **Truth** will leave no room for opinion.

**6** If **Truth** is your attorney, you will survive the trials of accusation.

**7** The wise interrogate rumor, the ignorant rumor.

---

**D i a m o n d    W o r d s**

*Howbeit when he, the Spirit of **Truth**, is come, he will guide you into all **Truth**: for he shall not speak of himself; but whatsoever he shall hear, that shall he speak: and he will show you things to come   John 16:13*

---

# Understanding

**①** **Understanding** is the tool the *Holy Spirit* uses to process "wisdom."

**②** You cannot **Understand** anothers position, until you can **Understand** anothers pain.

**③** Give others enough space to turn around, the same amount that you would need.

**④** Excellent people observe, average people react.

**⑤** You cannot **Understand** another's fears, until you can **Understand** another's failures.

**⑥** You will never **Understand** who you are, until you **Understand** why you are here.

**⑦** You will never **Understand** the power of "short term decisions," until you put everything through the "long range process."

---
D i a m o n d     W o r d s

*Wisdom is the principal thing; therefore get wisdom: and with all thy getting get* ***Understanding*** *Proverbs 4:7*

---

# Unity

**1** Revival does not happen when we all believe the same thing, it happens when we all "want" the same thing.

**2** **Unity** is the laying aside of common differences to pursue a common assignment.

**3** Just because someone is related, does not mean they are connected.

**4** **Unity** does not require you to agree with everything a person is before you can link with every place a person is going.

**5** When you identify what you need, who you need will emerge.

**6** You will never gain by one, what you can only gain with several.

**7** Never become involved with anything you don't believe in the end result of.

---

### D i a m o n d    W o r d s

*...Behold, how good and how pleasant it is for brethren to dwell together in **Unity**! Psalms 133:1*

# Vision

**1** If your **Vision** is not an obsession, it will never be a possession.

**2** You will never go beyond where you see yourself going.

**3** Never throw the pearls of your **Vision**, before the swine of opinions.

**4** If you don't believe in your **Vision**, what others believe about it will shake you.

**5** Your **Vision** will incorporate different people in different seasons. Celebrate the temporary as well as the permanent.

**6** Never defend your **Vision**, to those not assigned to be a part of it.

**7** **Vision** will require imagination for what is bigger than you are.

―――――― D i a m o n d    W o r d s ――――――

*Where there is no **Vision**, the people perish:*
*but he that keepeth the law, happy is he*
*Proverbs 29:18*

# Warfare

1. The object of **Warfare**, is to get someone bigger than your enemy to stand up on your battlefield.

2. The purpose of **Warfare** is to reap the bounty, not magnify the battle.

3. Every battle that *God* is not allowed to fight, you will have to.

4. **Warfare** begins with movement.

5. Never give opposition an explanation.

6. **Warfare** is the prelude to promotion.

7. When you maximize the size of your *God*, you minimize the size of your enemy.

---

### Diamond Words

*For in the time of trouble he shall hide me in his pavilion: in the secret of his tabernacle shall he hide me; he shall set me up upon a rock   Psalms 27:5*

# Weakness

**1** Never put yourself in a position where a **Weakness** is forced to defend you.

**2** What you do not conquer, will eventually conquer you.

**3** Never be transparent about your **Weaknesses**, to those incapable of strengthening them.

**4** **Weaknesses** require honesty more than diplomacy.

**5** **Weaknesses** are the reason *God* is still working in your life.

**6** **Weaknesses** are a reminder that pride has no platform.

**7** **Weaknesses** are the targets of perfection.

---

### Diamond Words

*To another faith by the same Spirit; to another the gifts of healing by the same Spirit*
*I Corinthians 12:9*

---

# Winning

**1** **Winning** is never possible, until the strategies for **Winning** are tangible.

**2** **Winners** never spend more time looking back on their next ones, than they do looking ahead to their next victories.

**3** You will never leave a losing season, until you get a photograph of a **Winning** one.

**4** Make a parade of your victories, more than a trail of your defeats.

**5** You will never have a **Winning** "Lifetime" until you have a **Winning** "Lifestyle."

**6** Humility is not the restriction from enjoying victory; it's the recognition of who enabled you to **Win**.

**7** You will only enjoy **Winning**, when you identify what is **Winning** for you!

---

D i a m o n d     W o r d s

*For thou, LORD, hast made me glad through thy work: I will triumph in the works of thy hands   Psalms 92:4*

---

# Word of God

**1** The **Word of God** is proof, *God* expects you to arrive at your destination.

**2** The **Word of God** will be a mirror that shows the "real you."

**3** Never apply partial scripture to justify whole error. Let the "Whole **Word**," be the "Whole Truth."

**4** *God* expects you to be so blessed, that *He* left you the map to the treasure.

**5** The miracles of **God's Word** are not stories to fascinate, they are examples to imitate.

**6** It's not until you interrogate the **Word of God**, that the curtain of truth opens wider.

**7** *God* thought enough of your questions, that *He* gave you a book with all the answers.

---

### Diamond Words

*Thy **Word** have I hid in mine heart, that I might not sin against thee   Psalms 119:11*

---

# Words

**1**▶ If something has no point, it has no purpose.

**2**▶ Those who are allowed to speak into your life, are allowed to decide your future.

**3**▶ When you embrace a person's **Words**, you embrace the motivations behind them.

**4**▶ Your "Vocabulary," reveals your focus.

**5**▶ People will never arrive at where you are, if you don't address them where they are.

**6**▶ Accurate **Words** leave you elevated above hearsay. Inaccurate **Words** leave you obligated to damage control.

**7**▶ Your **Words** will determine the level of change, that peoples lives experience.

---

────── D i a m o n d　　W o r d s ──────
*Hear; for I will speak of excellent things; and he opening of my lips shall be right things.*
*Proverbs 8:6*

# Worship

1. *God* responds to simplicity, before *He* recognizes ability, innocence before performance.

2. **Worship** is the only way you can control your environment, so contamination can't.

3. Victory in warfare is not why you **Worship**, it's the eventuality of your **Worship**.

4. When *God* is pleasured, there is nothing *He* can't do for you, and there is nothing your enemy can do against you.

5. True **Worship** is motivated by "Adoration," not bound by "Obligation."

6. A **Worshiper** is not a **Worshiper**, until they realize *God* knows everything about them and still loves them anyway.

7. True **Worship** is the purest form of gratitude that lets *God* know you love *Him* for who *He* is, more than for what *He* does.

---
D i a m o n d     W o r d s
---

*But the hour cometh, and now is, when the true **Worshippers** shall **Worship** the Father in spirit and in truth: for the Father seeketh such to **Worship** him   John 4:23*

# You

**❶** If **You** cannot be teachable, having a talent won't help **You**.

**❷** If **You** cannot be leadable, having a destination won't help **You**.

**❸** If **You** cannot be flexible, having a goal won't help **You**.

**❹** If **You** cannot be grateful, having abundance won't help **You**.

**❺** If **You** cannot be mentorable, having a future won't help **You**.

**❻** If **You** cannot be durable, having a plan won't help **You**.

**❼** If **You** cannot be reachable, having success won't help **You**.

---

Diamond   Words

*Before I formed thee in the belly I knew thee;
and before thou camest forth out of the womb
I sanctified thee, and I ordained thee a
prophet unto the nation   Jeremiah 1:5*

# Let Me Agree With You In Prayer For Your Need!

You are daily upon my heart and your needs matter greatly to me. Don't ever think that you are alone. I want to agree with you that the Holy Spirit will bring the provision of God in your life!

Name _____

Address _____

City _____ State _____ Zip _____

Phone ( )_____

**Clip & Mail To: Spirit & Life Ministries**
**P.O. BOX 41010    MINNEAPOLIS, MN 55441**

Clip & Mail

# More Power-Packed Teaching From J. Konrad Hölè

### The Leading Of His Spirit

Join J. Konrad for this "Explosive" and "In-Depth" study on how the Holy Spirit leads you more by "Purpose, Principals and Protocal" than He does by Euphoria, Emotion, and Excitement. The greatest seasons of your life are just ahead, LED BY HIS SPIRIT.
**$20.00 (4 tape series)**

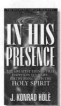

### In His Presence

Find out the life changing secrets of Kind David's revelation of how to live in the Presence of God. The most incredible breakthroughs in your life are about to take place just be being in His Presence.
**$15.00 (3 tape series)**

### Diary Of The Holy Spirit

Discover the benefits of how to Commune, Flow, Discern, and Listen to the Holy Spirit who Jesus said would be with you Always. Your greatest relationship is one revelation away.
**$15.00 (3 tape series)**

### Misery

Discover David's revelation principles from Psalms 16:11, that the only true place of joy was in God's presence, and that anything outside His presence was not designed to satisfy you, but rather would be a source of "Misery."
**$20.00 (4 tape series)**

### The Mentor And The Protege

What is a *Mentor*? A gift by *God* to insure the success of completing your *Assignment*. What is a *Protege*? A person whose future depends on the impartation from somebody who has already been where they are going. In this impactive teaching you will understand the purpose of mentoring.
**$20.00 (4 tape series)**

# "The Diamond Library For Achievers"
## Several Dynamic Topics:

## Build Your Complete Achiever Library!

### Obedience

Join J. Konrad for this "Impactive" study on the "Power" of OBEDIENCE and its ability to be the bridge from "Where You Are," to "Where You Want To Be ," and God's ability to react to your life everytime you follow one of "His Instructions."
**$10.00 (2 tapes)**

### Time

Join J. Konrad for this "Impactive" study on the "Currency of TIME," its ability to form your "Destiny" around you, and its critical role in developing your relationship with the Holy Spirit.
**$10.00 (2 tapes)**

### Focus

Join J. Konrad for this "Impactive" study on the Force of "FOCUS," and its ability to enable you to walk through the "Valleys of Distraction," and complete your life assignment!
**$10.00 (2 tapes)**

## Send Your Order In Today!

### Seed-Faith

Join J. Konrad for this "Impactive" study on the "Power Of Seed Movement" in your life, and your ability to take something God has placed in your hand, to create something God has ordained in your life.
**$10.00 (2 tapes)**

### Warfare

Join J. Konrad for this "Impactive" study of how you were not called to be a "Captive," you were called to be a "Deliverer."
**$10.00 (2 tapes)**

### Direction

Join J. Konrad for this "Impactive" study on how the "HOLY SPIRIT" answers one of the most pivotal questions ever in your life... the question of DIRECTION.!
**$10.00 (2 tapes)**

**SPECIAL PACKAGE PRICE... Receive all 6 titles into your life for just $30.** (please specify when ordering)

*Don't let these opportunities pass you by! Rush your order in today. Fill out the form below. Please print clearly and legibly. Ask the Holy Spirit what Seed He would have you to sow into this world-changing ministry.*

| Title | Qty. | Price | Total |
|---|---|---|---|
| The Leading Of His Spirit (Tapes) | | $ | $ |
| In His Presence (Tapes) | | $ | $ |
| The Diary Of The Holy Spirit  (Tapes) | | $ | $ |
| Misery (Tapes) | | $ | $ |
| The Mentor And The Protege (Tapes) | | $ | $ |
| Library For Achievers - Time (Tapes) | | $ | $ |
| Library For Achievers - Obedience (Tapes) | | $ | $ |
| Library For Achievers - Focus (Tapes) | | $ | $ |
| Library For Achievers - Seed-Faith (Tapes) | | $ | $ |
| Library For Achievers - Warfare (Tapes) | | $ | $ |
| Library For Achievers - Direction (Tapes) | | $ | $ |

1 Item.....................$2 - S/H     Shipping/Handling | $
2 Items ...................$3 - S/H     Seed-Faith Gift | $
3 or more Items.....$4 - S/H     Total | $

☐ J. Konrad, please send me my **FREE** copy of your *Spirit & Life Talk* newsletter.

☐ Check    ☐ Money Order    ☐ Visa    ☐ MasterCard

Card No. ☐☐☐☐☐☐☐☐☐☐☐☐☐☐☐☐

Exp. Date _____ Signature _____

Name _____

Address _____

City _____ State _____ Zip _____

Phone ( ____ ) _____

**Clip & Mail To: Spirit & Life Ministries**
**P.O. BOX 41010  MINNEAPOLIS, MN 55441**

Clip & Mail

*Choose From These Exciting Titles! Books that will bring a Breakthrough... Your life will be challenged and changed with revelation knowledge!*

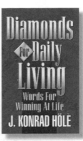

**Diamonds For Daily Living**

**Diamonds For Ministers**

**Diamonds For Mothers**

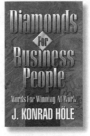

**Diamonds For Business People**

**You Were Born A Champion... Don't Die A Loser!**

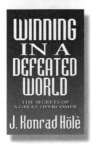

**Winning In A Defeated World**

**Leading In the Midst Of Followers**

**Living Large In A Small World**

**See the next page for details on how to order your personal copies of these books!**

# "Literature Evangelism Team"

## Order Form

☐ Yes, J. Konrad, I want to be a part of this "Evangelism Breakthrough" so that I may affect those that God links me to with the power of revelation knowledge.

*Order a set of 10 copies of any title for $10. You may also mix titles of the books to bring a total of 10 copies for $10. Order for your friends and family!*

| Title | Qty. (Sets of 10) | Price | Total |
|---|---|---|---|
| Diamonds For Daily Living | | x $10 | $ |
| Diamonds For Ministers | | x $10 | $ |
| Diamonds For Mothers | | x $10 | $ |
| Diamonds For Business People | | x $10 | $ |
| You Were Born A Champion... | | x $10 | $ |
| Winning In A Defeated World | | x $10 | $ |
| Leading In The Midst Of Followers | | x $10 | $ |
| Living Large In A Small World | | x $10 | $ |
| Add $2 For Shipping | Shipping | | $ |
| | Seed-Faith Gift | | $ |
| | Total | | $ |

☐ Check   ☐ Money Order   ☐ Visa   ☐ MasterCard

Card No. ☐☐☐☐☐☐☐☐☐☐☐☐☐☐☐☐

Exp. Date _____ Signature _____

Name _____

Address _____

City _____ State _____ Zip _____

Phone ( ) _____

**Clip & Mail To: Spirit & Life Ministries**
P.O. BOX 41010   MINNEAPOLIS, MN 55441

*Clip & Mail*